...c

...asilook...

Volume One

...markanthonythomas...

...markanthonythomas...

Library of Congress Cataloging-in-Publication Data

Printed August 2000

ISBN – 0-9703649-0-3

Additional copies and information about this book can be requested at
www.markanthonythomas.com

Publisher:

Amazing Experiences Press
1908 Keswick Lane
Concord, California 94518

- Cover Illustration, Layouts and Design all created by Mark Anthony Thomas
- Photos by Ernest Dean Thomas II
- Biography Photo courtesy of University of Georgia Department of Communications and The Arch Society

This book is respectfully dedicated to the memory of

Earnestine Whimper

(1933- 1994)

(R.I.P.) Rejoice In Paradise

Acknowledgments

...First and foremost, I must thank God for giving me the talent, the strength, and the desire to express myself artistically. Lord, you are the foundation and the owner of all my talents and you are worthy of all the praise. As I Look is a culmination of achievement, disappointment, hurt, love, self-discovery, and many, many other issues that young adults in the 21st century deal with. Each piece of work – although it may not directly reflect my life – has significance to my experience within my 21 years of existence. But throughout my years, there have been numerous people who helped shape me to be "who I am" in 2000. Mom and Dad - who raised me well – thanks! Being a single mom wasn't easy, but with God, you did it Ma. The Thomas-Whimper family, what can I say? I love ya'll and you have been a support system – although I didn't appreciate it until after I entered college – for years and I treasure every moment that we've shared. Ernest, Darius, and Devin, I have worked hard to be your motivation, so don't derail from the road to success. Bianca thanks for being the great sister you are.

...Grandma Earnestine helped mold my views, personality, and encouraged me to be the giving, sensitive and loving person I am today. "If only she would have lived to see the potential I had in me!" I miss her dearly - although it's been years - but this is my repayment for her motivation and strength. The first poem I remember writing – in 2nd grade - was dedicated to her, therefore my first book will be too.

...When I began work on this project, there was one person who lived with me and served as a mentor during the process – Bryant Baugh. Love you man and thanks for being the un-official "editor" of ...asilook... Tiana, you're my best friend in the world and God knows I'd do everything to protect you from any hurt, harm, or danger. Thanks for being the motivation for my motivational pieces. Let's step back to high school – where the poetry began. Thanks Ms. Knowles – for your inspiration, Mrs. Jackson, for your dedication, Mrs. Fuller, for everything, and Mrs. Blair, for being you. Mrs. Davidson, thanks for helping me develop my writing skills and Mr. Mansor, thanks for giving me a forum to share my works. Principal Bro. Mack, "brother, you" were the role model for everybody. Then, there's Holy Fellowship C.O.G.I.C. Thanks Elder and Sister Paden for your

commitment. Sister Williams, Wanda, Sister George, Mother Ringer, and everyone, I love you all dearly and I appreciate your support.

...Now, UGA, where do I begin? Brothers, Brothers, Brothers - thanks for all of your support. From Four M.E.N. to Seven Heirs, where do I begin? LBs (2x, Jarmon, Chris Soji, and Trent), thanks for your support through the hardest times of my life. You guys know the true "story within" - that even the wisest readers won't get. Seven Heirs, I couldn't have asked for a greater class to be a fraternal father for. Preston, Tavares, Lance and Jay, thanks for actively supporting my work and talent. Don Weston, Rick Blalock, Skip Mason, Darrell Ray, Walt Kimbrough, Brent Swinton, and Rudy Williams, you all are my older brothers within Alpha. I appreciate your continued support for my work and everything else I attempt to do. Mia M., Jessica L., Monet, Kezia, Chansi, Karen, Mark M., Lashonda, and Kellee Ross, you all have been supporting my work from day one and I told you I wouldn't forget it. Neusomba, thanks for being a great friend and labeling my work "Mark Anthony Thomas quality." Carmen, Allison, and Nicole, my three big sisters at Georgia, you didn't have to be who you were for me, but you were. Kim B., Vanessa, and Miss Shirley, thanks for letting me express my "story within" for thousands - you are all a blessing to everyone. Thanks to Kim Wuenker and the Arch Society.

...Jeri, you were and are the greatest and I'll always remember the motivation you gave me during my trial as the "first." Tameka, thanks for helping me wrap things on this project up. Perry, sorry you missed so much, but now you have the chance to have a role in my role in life...thanks for all you do, I love you and appreciate you being who you are for me. It takes a village to raise a child and it takes many influences to shape a man. Thanks to the Atlanta Braves for recognizing my talent in front of thousands as their 1997 English Scholar. Thanks, for hunting me down to give me the award when I forgot to put my address on the essay. I'm an eternal fan for life. I'm very appreciative and take nothing for granted. For all those who have made contributions to my endeavors, I thank you and I pray that God will bless you. Now, its time for you to see what I've produced, take a look...

...order...of...appearance...

...order...of...appearance...

...asilook at the backbone of my vitality...
...asilook at the hurt and success...
...asilook at my pilgrimage through reality...
...asilook at all spiritual tests...

PRELUDE

...the confession booth...

take a seat,
look closely,
listen, conceive,
as I confess,
disclose,
reveal,
but most importantly
- expressing openly -
and keeping it real,
my...

(1)

That's Deep

**What makes a man deep?
Is it the fact that his thoughts transcend
the depths of the mental capacity,
Or is he utilizing the capacity of his creativity to make us think that his expectations surmount the limitations of our minds?
But does that make him deep?
...Well look at it like this, you can think you're deep –
and be as deep as the water in the broken pool of a child
– making you really wafer thin and puddle shallow -
But you'll have the nerves to still claim that you're deep.
Then, you have the commercial deep.
See people thinks these folks are deep and they'll
Ride the fame of the title all the way to the heaven of hype,
Not realizing that they're caught up in a purgatory
of self-indulgence, and suffer from the expectation of expectation...
...But, that doesn't mean they're not deep?
Hell, You got a Nikki Gamma. an Edgar Rho. and Langston Eta. -
three filters for the common man compiled with those who commercially lift their founder – while the great one
celebrates what their creativity innovates.
But then, we can't forget the wanna-be-deeps,
who decorate themselves like Christmas trees –
With colorful ornaments and eccentricities –
Not realizing that their beneficiaries...
...will look back and smirk at when mama and papa tried too hard
to be too cool, but really looked like a damn fool
and now they have the nerves to tell us
what we can and shouldn't do,
Shaping conflict after conflict – because they were caught up in
The conflict of trying too hard to go deep...
And they don't want you to repeat, their mistakes.
But you haven't answered my question, am I deep?...
...How 'bout you flow down my shallow river,
Which will lead you down my lake of forte,
And you'll levitate in my ocean of intellectual paragons,
And while you sway back and forth – in my liquid of innovative yet
borderline psychotic thoughts - tell me if you'll stay afloat.**

(2)

Encourage Me

Aim me,
like an arrow,
And I will score within my goal.
Inspire me,
in every way and just watch
my life's success story unfold.
Encourage me,
just like a child
to do what's right every time.
Criticize me,
constructively,
and you'll see prosperity be mine.
Fabricate my
self esteem and
understand how I truly feel.
Guide my paths,
the best way you can,
and my allegiance will
be revealed.
Enlighten me,
when I don't comprehend,
so I will know what's
right from wrong.
And please,
Remember me,
when I depart and
I'll be thankful
for you,
when I'm gone.

(3)

The Night That Jesus Came

The night that my Jesus came,
I heard a blaring sound.
For I awoke and started yelling
from fear, as I fell to the ground.
Then I saw The Luminous Glare
- so bright that I closed my eyes.
As the endangered Earth trembled
my body slowly began to rise.
But then, I reopened my eyes
as I saw His breathtaking face.
- This crystal clear vision was just too hard to erase.
I fell back on the ground and said, "Oh Lord please forgive."
He said, "My child you've done well, eternal life you shall live!"
I started to praise our Lord, asilook-ed at the scars he bared.
From when he died on Calgary to show me how much he cared.
He said, "Child say not a word, while I will guide you and protect."
And being the person that I am, I just couldn't disrespect.
He said, "Come with me my child,
It's time for us to go.
And the place where you'll spend eternity,
I'm sure that you should know."
We traveled above the earth and
were parallel to all His stars,
He turned and smiled at me and
said, "Heaven, here we are."
The streets were all paved with gold
and all my troubles were gone away.
I saw my loved ones that passed,
for this was my remarkable day.
For obeying His holy word,
He said I'd get my reward.
He looked at me and grinned and
said, "Heaven is completely yours."
I started jumping and shouting
because my life wouldn't
be the same.
The night I would eternally remember,
The night that my Jesus came.

(4)

When Jesus Turned His Back On Me

I turned my back on Jesus,
So he turned his back, On me.
And when he turned,
My soul burned with guilt,
For my eyes saw the scars,
That he bared,
And the pain of mine,
That he shared,
And I saw the days,
When I gave up,
But he,
Still cared,
And showed me that
My suffering was not unfair...
...presented through these scars,
These scars inflicted,
when he took credit,
credit for my sins,
And co-signed with God,
To give me a chance,
A chance at life again.

(5)

. . . away, away, away Away away, away, away . . .

I was only a child in the womb and
never saw the break of day.
But it never entered my thoughts
That 'you' would take my life away.
From the moment I came to be,
I always had faith in 'you.'
Hoping to see your beautiful face,
But now, my existence is through.
The tears 'you' cried, I heard,
I felt all the suffering 'you' had.
I didn't think that me being here,
Was only making 'you' mad.
Well, I am sorry for being formed,
There is nothing else I can even say.
Still, why did 'you' have to do it?
'You' threw my whole life away.
'You' never gave me a chance,
So 'you' did what 'you' thought was right.
'You' say that 'you' had not one regret,
But why couldn't 'you' sleep that night?
I lived such a trivial life,
For, I was aborted on this biased day.
Just tell me what inspired 'you,'
To take my precious life away,
away,
away,
away,
away,
away...

(6)

Part of You

I'm the image in your photo,
I'm the reason that you are you,
I'm the power in your electricity,
You are part of me, And I'm part you.
I'm the atmosphere for your earth,
The vision in your imagery,
I'm the beat and rhymes in your music,
I'm your model for your way things should be.
I'm the drive for your aspiration,
The goal for your destination,
The argument in your instigation,
The shortness in your abbreviation,
I'm the uniqueness in your originality,
The privacy in your sexuality,
The 'fakeness' in your congeniality,
I'm the mistiness in your blue,
I'm the hope when you made it through,
I'm the escapade in your rendezvous,
I am a defining part of you, a vital part of you,
I am the will in everything you do,
You are part of me, and I'm part of you.

INTERLUDE

...game of taboo...

the phrase: "the black man"
struggled,
denied,
dismissed,
stereotyped,
endangered,
misunderstood

(7)

My Journey With Six Pharaohs

The first Pharaoh, The ace, the rock
His name is "me,"
The one they said everyone would see,
The first point of the line,
shortest, but the mastermind.
Had the heart to stick to the fight,
And gain the strength to lead more and more each night.
On his journey with six Pharaohs,
He kept his head and pushed ahead.
"When the flames of death burned down,
and the smoke cleared away,
there stood seven new Pharaohs,
that were in it to stay."

Pharaoh number two,
wise, let me reprise, when I needed help,
He was there, When I was down,
He destroyed my despair.
At his place, Is where we halted our race,
He's unique, with wit, but refused to quit.

Pharaoh number three,
Wears his number with dignity,
physically strong,
No doubts to press on, quiet but energetic,
Someone trying to hurt me,
Ohh, he won't have it,
The brother we all need,
with eyes searching to succeed.

Pharaoh number four,
Should I say more?
Intellect, but sometimes a fool,
But that's what makes him the definition of cool.
Makes me laugh,
And I'd give him anything I have.
Loves and won't hesitate to fight,
but stayed on point each night.
My actions and smile reveal,
the admiration towards him I feel...

Pharaoh number five,
Straight-up Live, My #5,
What can I say?
Special in every way, Cool and concerned,
as we grow and learn, and reached our goal,
We promised that our
friendship would uphold.
Strong, careful, and so analytical.
He'll make an extra effort to stay sincere.
That why respect for him is first tier.

Pharaoh number six,
A man with a heart, And much love to share,
Sincere and smart,
And always shows that he cares.
Overprotective, just a bit,
but pressed on more with every hit.
Adored by everyone,
As for our line, he's the distinct one.

Pharaoh number seven,
The tail of our cast, but no where near last.
Everyone should know,
that this man can steal the show.
His number is special to us all,
For he stands more than just tall.
He's cool, sometimes a fool,
Never paused to rest,
he's simply the best.

The Seven Pharaohs of Eternal Phire,
Kept the strength to pursue
and undeniable desire.
Our journey was hard,
but we refused to give up,
let go, and give in.
And, when I was down, I always had
six shoulders to lend.

(8)

Brother, You

If I was to create the model brother,
I would use all the ingredients of you.
Someone every young
black male needs in their life,
A role model with goals, of you.
When I see how successful you've become,
My heart fills with admiration for you.
Standing strong and stoic against all inhibitions,
My inspiration brother, you.
You probably don't realize how "bad" you are,
Look at the way we magnify and thank you.
Prosperity and visions
written all over your face,
My motivation brother, you.
If you walk through one of the many prisons,
You'll see brothers, that look like me and you.
But, the world should know more
success stories like yours,
My respect brother, for you.
If you ever get discouraged
by the many hardships,
Let my assurance inspire you.
Continue to mesmerize and attract all eyes,
And keep it real dynamic brother, yes you.

...asilook at my attempt to achieve...
...asilook at my respect for manhood...
...asilook at my experience to initiate...
...asilook at the will to do good...

(9)

What ANYONE Could Do...

ANYONE could have done it,
But NO ONE wanted to.
But SOMEONE could have only done,
What EVERYONE knew they could do.

When NO ONE wanted to do it,
EVERYONE was doing something else.
If only SOMEONE would have done it.
Instead they cared about only themselves.

EVERYONE knew that they were able to do it,
But NO ONE would stand up and be that ONE.
Since NO ONE would volunteer to do it,
NO ONE did what ANYONE could have done.

So if NO ONE wants to do it,
Then YOU stand up and be that SOMEONE.
Because ANYONE can set a sincere example,
And be the leader for EVERYONE.

(10)

The Story Within

When you look at
the significance of my achievements...
You may see the school where I'll commence,
The trinities of my name,
The dates when my dreams came true,
The concentration I'll forever claim...
However...
You won't see the days when I wanted to quit,
The doubts that entered my mind,
The goal that was an eternity away,
The times when I felt I was losin' my mind...
You won't see...
The stories of days that swiftly passed,
The times I needed our celestial Friend,
The tests and triumphs that college brings,
You won't see the story that lies within.
You won't see...
The tears that departure day brought,
The loan the University wouldn't give,
The nights that I'm still tryin' to forget,
And beggin' daddy for money mama couldn't give.
You won't see...
The everlasting brothers and sisters I've found,
The report that had HOPE no where in sight,
The times I couldn't do nothin' but curse,
The days when only hurdles were in sight.
You definitely won't see...
The results the doctor didn't have to say,
The stab wounds of betrayal on my back,
The pain of the love ones that passed away,
The days when insecurities were holding me back.
So,
When you look at my epitomes of succeeding,
Look for the story of triumph that lies deep in,
For my success represents more that the eye can see,
But challenges conquered,
My story within.

(11)

In Shackles

The foundation that
this country was built on,
Was that everyone
shall have liberty.
Just tell me who
gave you the right,
To take the freedom
that was given to me?
You shackled me
like a vicious criminal,
In chains when my
life had just begun.
I never got to
see my lonely mother
And my father
never held his only son.
I work so hard
from dusk to dawn,
And I rarely
get time to rest.
And whenever I
disobey you master,
You slash scars
across my chest.
You beat me
like a stubborn child
But, I never cry
or attempt to fight.
These scars symbolize
my agony and pain,
And you know that
this horror isn't right.
I've attempted many
times to run
away but you stopped me dead in my tracks.
I was forced to return to this horrible nightmare,
And had a whip slashed across my back.
I pray to God that he'll save me,
For my trouble and hurt he'll always see.
Life in these shackles I refuse to spend another day,
'Cause master, I am setting myself free.

INTERLUDE

...running...

running?
where you're gonna run?
you can't run from me
"I'm your pain"
I'm an evil god and you'll carry me
to each destination
and I'll continue to
instigate, aggravate
and resentment,
I'll create
between you
and
your soul
because eventually
you'll see
that you're aren't bold
enough to
deal with me

(12)

What if

What if I crumble?
And let all the feelings inside,
Open wide my emotions...
And pour down to my
Zone of comfort,
And burn through the shield protecting my pride,
And defrost a window for the world to see
Inside the secrets...
The hidden thoughts...
the blueprint defining "who I am?"
And what makes me, me?

(13)

Doing Nothing

Asilook-ed at him brutally and mentally abusing her,
I just stood there,
watching, thinking,
but, doing nothing.
Asilook-ed at the man
begging for money to eat,
I just stood there,
selfishly, unobservant,
doing nothing.
Asilook-ed at them
unmercifully being thrashed,
I just stood there,
vacant, emotionless,
doing nothing but thinking,
"it is not my problem,"
until,
I was the one, in their shoes,
by myself, being hurt,
while others, stood there,
vacant, emotionless,
unabashed,
apathetic,
selfishly,
unobservant
and
they did nothing to save me....

...asilook at my repression and resentment...
...asilook at my risks to gain...
...asilook at her departure and the aftermath...
...asilook at the mental and physical strain...

(14)

WOUNDS

Wound one,
Wound two,
and
Wound three
are all stitched up.
Wound four
is when all that pain
Supposedly drained.
Wound five,
Is internal,
In the heart of my brain.
Wound five runs so deep,
the ocean couldn't hide it.
It contains so much anger,
That even Hitler would stamp it "evil."
It contains so much sin,
That the devil would call it wrong.
It contains so much damn pain,
That even an aborted child
Wouldn't trade its place to feel the anguish.
The fifth wound had an
Excessive growth of
weeks and months of continuous
stress and hurt, and grief
and anger, and ridicule
as well as misery
and damn stress
and regret, and shit
and pain...
Which hardened and froze
But, you still stitched up the wound?
But, regardless of how long
the stitches stay in -
Or how many times you said
the stitches would trap all the blood that
continued to leak my pain and resentment -
The wound just won't heal.

INTERLUDE

...don't return...

you are opening my portal of resentment,
my thoughts of damnation,
passing through my wound
of everlasting depression,
so don't leave offended,
don't leave with an
uninvited predisposition,
just make sure you leave,
and like me, don't return...

(15)

Ohh God

"Ohh God, Why?"

Why have you left me in this pain? Why have you abandoned me to mold insane? Why haven't you showed me a sign that you're there?
Or shipped a revelation to show you care? Why I am in the place that I am? Or why do I feel you don't give a damn?
Why am I tangled in the realm of sin?
And how did I reach the state of mind that I'm in?
Lord, when will my prior happiness return? Is this all a lesson I forgot to learn? I always knew that it would soon be my turn
To test my soul, to see it will forever burn... In a world called hell,
Which is the way I honestly feel... Caught only in this mess and these unforeseen ordeals... And does anyone understand what's in my head? Or feel the pain when I cry to myself in bed?
I know my folks are worried inside, while other folks are concerned if I'll mentally survive? God, It just can't be my fault that I'm in this state? And will the light that I reach be eternally great?
Why haven't you showed me a sign that you're there?
Or called me to tell me that you're there? Or just said, "Child I'm still here?" Ohh God, I need to know you're still there?
Why I am in the place that I am?
Or why do I feel you don't give a damn?

(16)

Un-Due

Un-fill my recollections with anger, Un-pour resentment into my heart.
Un-attach me to this newfound situation, And Un-break my spirit apart.
Un-toss me in the mist of that horror, Un-tell all the lies that you said.
Un-promise to take care of me,
And Un-instill thoughts of rather being dead.
Un-emphasize your frivolous reasons, Un-allow this hurt to continue to remain.
Un-abuse me all the ways that you did, and please, if possible,
Un-due this, un-due this, un-due this...

(17)

Soliloquy

You lied,
But you haven't cried
Personally I don't think you
even tried to find a way
To say what you wanted to say
And regardless, it was all a
lie, *to cover this mess*
And now you won't be able to rest
And live with these lies on top
of your chest
And you knew the best
Thing to do was to reveal *your pain*
And not let your esteem take
the drain
Because no one can train
to be in your place
And not let the *confusion* show on your face
For you control this race
and don't you think the lies *may trace*
back to you
and then, what are you going to do
will you be able to make it through
or will you *look them in the eyes and say*
fuck all of ya'll, I don't want *this*
But something inside won't let you un-list
Is it the goal that you can't resist
When inside you want to say kiss
my...*and go back to your old* life
And put down this *self* aimed knife

INTERLUDE

...re-creation...

we're undergoing a re-creation,
after the extensive
annihilation,
eradication,
humiliation,
and
elimination
of my soul.
so, don't be
disappointed,
don't say a damn word,
if you don't like the new people
I've become

(18)

Journey To The Center of the Earth

I was faced with troubles at home
and ran into troubles at school,
I was weak. Weak as a premature child
Two seconds from death...
See, I was faced with these troubles to soon,
For my mind and my emotions were too premature,
To face what I had to endure...I was weak...Too weak to walk,
So I couldn't travel to the sanctuary,
For I was buried in trouble, covered in hurdles of disparity,
And no one's help and charity
Could make me feel like I was worth a dime,
I grabbed a shovel,
With my weak back and sore mind
And used all the energy that I could find,
To dig...Dig between the earth
to find the roots of my pain...as I dug, I found water,
which provide nourishment to reach my destiny.
I dug past the crust of the earth...with its solid shield,
And the heat of the center of the Earth,
my body could slowly feel...

...then, I reached the inner-core, and the heat of the Earth
Slowly pierced my core.
As the heat of the Earth penetrated my mind,
It burned away the pain - which helped me find...
That hidden motivation for gain,
And it made me stronger, harder, realer
And more capable to handle,
The things I was too weak to endure...
And I landed straight in the center of the Earth,
The center of all, the center of
God's creation for God's creations,
Which help me discover the creation of my pain,
The creation of my struggle,
Which shifted me back through the creation of the stronger me,
The creation of motivation within me,
And propelled me towards best man I could be...

...asilook at moving on and letting love...
...asilook at the many ways to cope...
...asilook at the sorrow and tranquillity...
...asilook at fondness, devotion and hope...

(19)

Too Different

we're just too, too different!!!
if...
we're two different people,
with two different minds,
and two different goals,
on two different boats,
in two different seas,
going two different ways,
on two different planets,
in two different galaxies,
in two different universes,
under two different gods...
why do I feel we're meant to be?

(20)

Without

My love sat next to me and looked
At me with her vibrant smile.
And then she said,
"It's like...
A heart without a beat.
No life it can provide
And no feeling deep down inside."
She paused and said,
"It's like...
A face without emotions.
No smile to convey
And nothing positive to ever say."
She looked deep in my eyes and said,
"It's like...
A mind without thoughts.
Just emptiness within,
No thoughts of the one you love and friends."
Then, she started laughing and said,
"It's like...
Man without God.
No one trustworthy for you to lend,
Or parameters for your urges to sin."
And she started to grin as
a tear fell from her eye,
Then she said,
"It's like...
Me without you.
No one to love and devote my life,
Or even hold and become your wife.
For you converge my joy with happiness,
And overflowed heaven in my emptiness.
'Cause you are the love that lives in me,
And without you my love, I wouldn't be.
And you should know that I'll always be true,
Because I am nothing,
without you."

(21)

360

Her hips curve like a 360 --- encircling my fantasies,
My dreams, My wills to please...
And makes me weak in the knees,
As her wealth and assets,
Are asking me to invest,
In her happiness...
And calling for me,
To be the man she needs,
To help her fulfill her womanly deeds
And drive channels of desire
Through every inch of her existence --- and complete her circle.

INTERLUDE

...record player...

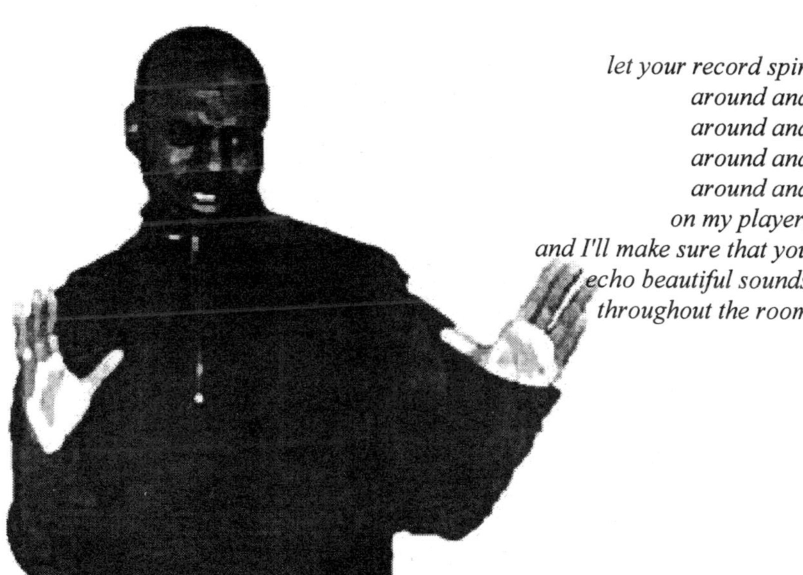

let your record spin
around and
around and
around and
around and
on my player,
and I'll make sure that you
echo beautiful sounds
throughout the room

(22)

Spinning Around

My world is spinning around
And around and around,
Hoping that when
it stops,
You will be at the center of my heart,
The equator of my existence...
Giving you every molecule of my love,
From pole to pole...
And when you touch me for the first time,
my world will rotate around your light,
For you are the sun,
For which my smile shines,
And have the gravitational pull,
To all the thoughts of my mind...
And you spin around my intentions,
Each night and day...and I pray,
that when my world stops spinning,
Your arms will be opened - facing my way.

(23)

Too scared to close my eyes

I'm too scared to close my eyes,
Because the question marks of confusion,
And bubbles of disappointment
May convert to tears and run down my face.
I'm too scared to close my eyes...
Because the love I let build may break into pieces
And fall so hard against my soul,
That it will create reminding bruises and scars
To send impulses of pain up my spine,
I'm too scared to close my eyes...
Because I can appear as things are fine,
When my smile hides true feelings inside,
And naturally shows my emotions' disguise,
And protects her remorseful, yet innocent heart,
From feeling apart of the reason why...
I'm too scared to close my eyes.

(24)

My Excuse

Saturated in loneliness,
I am dying...but you give me an excuse to find
An outlet for my remoteness,
To find the emancipation for my seclusion.
I have an excuse to be an addict,
So I can overdose on the killers of pain
- and point the finger at you,
right? Because you're my excuse.
I can pour spirits into my consciousness - and claimed you
were my barless-tender who continued to fill my cups for me to drink
away my reasons to not mourn.
I can divide into multiple personalities and have a soul-civil war,
And say you were the foundation for the fights to begin.
After all, you were my excuse, right?
Be my reason to just nut-up,
flatten someone's tires and make appearances
In a psychiatrist's chair.
Be my justification to turn dysfunctional and bizarre and
Send me on journeys to discover myself,
when I already knew who I was.
You won't be my woman, You won't be my soul mate,
You won't be the greatest thing that could happen to my life,
So at least be something, be something, so be my excuse.

(25)

When The Rain (Turns Into Snow)

When the joyful holiday season arrives,
That's when my pain and solitude show.
Because I think about you most of all
When the rain turns into snow.
During the springtime those memories fade,
And I'm able to bury my tears.
When the May flowers begin to bloom,
Their beauty always comforts my fears.
And when the summer sun echoes its energy,
The pleasure overshadows your glow.
While the world enjoys its warmer days,
I appear energetic and seasonal.
But those memories start to reappear,
After autumn leaves its mark.
For its cooler air makes me long for your love
And blows emptiness straight to my heart.
As I watch the rain convert to snow,
That's when it's harder to let you go.
My thoughts of your departure
Begin to reappear, when the rain turns into snow.
Your memories are so dear to me,
And the hurt will always show.
I miss you most when the warmth disappears,
When the rain turns into snow.

(26)

THE REASON

Who?
"I only knew her as Christine."
What?
"We made passionate love, if you know what I mean."
When?
"It was me and my girl's three month anniversary."
Where?
"At Motel 6, Room 166, I rented a room for one night,
After me and my girl had this stupid fight,"
Why?
"When I asked my girl to make love she said, "Sweetheart it's too soon."
I angrily replied, "I've waited 3 months, it's our anniversary, We can make love right now upstairs in your room."
She said,

"But, I'm a virgin and you know I'm not ready
To go all the way."
I said,
"Don't tell me that shit!
I have needs and I can't wait another day."
She started to cry and said,
"Baby, I thought you understood,"
I said,
"I do! I grabbed my stuff,
Jumped in my ride and I cruised through the neighborhood."
Then,
There was Christine,
One of the easy local girls,
And she crept over to my ride,
She said,
"Looking good tonight!"
And she opened the door
And eased inside."
How?
"She started smiling at
Me and I knew what
Was on her mind.
And,
I didn't care who it was,
Because tonight,
I was getting mine.
We approached the hotel,
And I quickly checked in.
Once we got into the
Bedroom,
Our night of lust would soon begin,
There was,
kissin', back scratchin',
huggin', hair pullin',
and all that good stuff.
And then,
Without a shield,
I began to penetrate,
And her body started
To marinate and,
As hours passed,
It was over."
Years later,
This is the story I told my doctor.

...asilook at life through the eyes of a child...
...asilook at my aggressive mind...
...asilook at relaxation and the good days...
...asilook misfortune within other's time...

(27)

When One Equals Two

Mommy loves Daddy,
And Daddy loves Mommy.
But last night, I awoke at 2:06 on that Tuesday morning,
And I heard Mommy and Daddy fighting.
Immediately scared, I ran into
Mommy and Daddy's room.
Suddenly, I saw Daddy hit Mommy with his fist.
Mommy's face started bleeding,
And I started crying as I saw the
Blood run down Mommy's face.
Mommy started crying and using bad words.
She told Daddy to get out and
she slapped Daddy and ran into the kitchen.
I followed them and asked Daddy not
to hurt Mommy, as I cried.
Mommy said a bad word to me
and I knew that she was mad.
Mommy picked up the phone and called
the police, But Daddy knocked the
phone out of her hand.
Mommy reached in the drawer and pulled
out a knife and aimed it at Daddy.
"Don't Mommy, don't hurt Daddy," I said.
She didn't listen.
Mommy told me to go to bed and I saw Daddy grabbing for Mommy.
But, it was too late. As Daddy grabbed,
Mommy stabbed,
and stabbed,
and stabbed,
and stabbed,
and stabbed.
I screamed, and screamed,
But Mommy didn't stop.
Instantly, I lost Daddy,
And, When the police came,
I lost Mommy,
Two.

(28)

when i needed u

**when i needed a shoulder to cry on,
when i needed someone to dry my eyes.
when i needed someone to stand by me,
u suddenly said, "goodbye."
when i took my very first step,
when i learned to tie my first shoe.
when i saw my very first day of school,
where were u when i needed u?
when i said my very first words,
when i got into my very first fight.
when i had no one to comfort me,
i just cried to myself at night.
when i had my first endeavor,
when i needed real help from u.
or just when i needed a true good friend,
u weren't there when i needed u.
when i didn't understand my homework,
or even when i first fell in love.
i always wondered since u weren't there,
was it my feeling u were thinking of?
i never understood why u left me,
i was your child and u departed away.
i wish u were there when i needed u,
but instead u went astray.
i hope that u never forget me,
after all u never showed me u cared.
so when u ask me do i remember u.
i'll reply, "i remember u were never there."**

(29)

RACE

We started at the same point.
We took off at the same time.
We ran at the same speed to the goal,
But his timer was somewhat different than mine.
When we reached the destination,
the results showed the anticipated tie.
But, why on Earth do they continue to feel
superior to you and I???

(30)

Hurt, Forever

Late... Approaching.... Park.... Traveling.... Home....Late....Tired.... Unaware.... Suddenly.... Males.... Appeared.... Two....Rude.... Aggressive.... Strong.... Pulled.... Alone.... Screamed.... Slapped.... Undressed.... Penetrated.... Unassisted.... Alone.... Painfully.... Scarred.... Mentally.... Physically.... Socially.... Hurt.... Alone.... Abandoned....Bleeding.... Dirty.... Unclean.... Rejected.... Traveling.... Alone.... Crying....Praying.... Scarred.... Forever, forever,,,

(31)

MyStory

I want to disclose how I feel because
the misery I cause I can see.
Just understand,
I'm not the one to blame - as you listen to my story.
See, people use my strength to protect themselves
and they look at me and feel fear.
But, I have no input for the trouble I cause,
and my oblivious heart stays sincere.
I'm used to abuse and kidnap
and cause widespread disintegration.
Humanity uses me to destroy itself,
And hinders contemplation.
I am used redundantly, in a time of war,
But can be used to set victims free.
Just know, I have no control,
as I divulge to you my story.
People are resting in their death bed, courtesy of me,
When it was well before their time.
Children are exterminated by me, excessively,
And a reason I just can't find.
I am used to steal, compelled to kill,
and regret this life everyday.
When I look in the eyes of my many victims,
Oh, the apologies I desire to say.
I'm disliked, forbidden, and even hated
by some, And all this heartache
I cause just shouldn't be.
But, do not condemn me for my deplorable life,
This painful life is
MyStory.

INTERLUDE

...hide 'n' seek...

let's play a game
of hide 'n' seek.
How about
we hide our pain,
and seek it later

(32)

A New Poem

A New Song,
An account from the
heart of someone deep in thought,
A New Mind,
Taking advantage of
the gift that your Savior bought.
A New Love,
Attracted to the beauty that lies within,
A New Goal,
A vision in life were you don't always win.
A New Idea,
Using your creativity to originate,
A New Child,
Offspring of what God and love can make.
A New Heart,
Realizing that all pain won't last forever,
A New Friend,
Creating a bond that
triumphs each endeavor.
A New Poem,
A compilation of exhales from a writer's mind,
A New Day,
Hope that happiness is what you'll find.
A New Home,
A place where many
memories will soon form,
A New Wish,
Aspirations to achieve far above the norm.

(33)

You, You, and You

I have this little problem.
I'm tangled in love and tied up between You, You, And You.
See You make me feel like You're the one.
But baby You give me nothing but dedication.
But still, why are my thoughts always
Centered around You.
What's a man like me to do?
When he's tied up between You, You, and You.
Because You don't understand...See, If I choose You,
Then, I'll loose You and You.
But, why is it that when I'm with You,
I envision myself with You?
But, when I'm loving You,
Why am I fantasizing about pleasing You?
What's a man to do?
When he's tied up between You, You, and You?
See I can write a million words just on You,
But, I can dance around the world for You,
But, when it all adds up,
My mind just can't stay off of You,
What's a man like me to do,
When he's tangled in love
and tied up between You, You and You.

(34)

The Wall

**The place we gather
To share stories of days that swiftly pass.
The spot where we
Enhance friendships that will forever last.
The place for each of us
to publicize.
The spot for everyone to realize...
That the wall is more than just a wall.
It is a destination,
A goal,
Future stories to be told.
A common ground for us all,
In a place where
we're surrounded by them all.**

...asilook at the fun and the fantastic...
...asilook at questioning my faith...
...asilook at my influence and my challenges...
...asilook at other's attempts to halt my race...

(35)

Out

I'm going out!
I'm throwing on some
party clothes..
hanging in the loops,
lacing up the boots,
gonna get rid of these tired blues
'cause, I'm going out.
Calling my bruhs...
heading to the spot...
girls a twurking, this place is hot...
I dance with some ladies...
get in the groove...
Uh oh...that's my song...
time to break out
the "smooth," "the train,"
and other party moves...
after we set it off,
even folks not dancing
are at the bar gettin' off,
it makes me not want to go
back in...
cause reality will return,
with lessons to learn,
disadvantages to burn...
and problems to concern.
But, until the DJ kicks me out,
or the police say
"get the hell out,"
or a fight makes everyone dip out.
I'm staying out, cause I'm not about
sit up in the house with nothing to do,
When I don't have to sit
around feelin' blue.

(36)

Saturday Night

It's Saturday night...are you ready to get drunk,
or as you would say krunk?
After all, it's time to make arrangements to have a good time,
beautiful ladies all willing to be yours and mine -
at least tonight man, this Saturday night...But you know it's official early Sun-
day morning...you don't wanna hear that though,
so I won't mention that fact,
cause it might bring you back,
to your senses...The night passes by,
like trains in a quiet southern village,
We're slowly recuperating from our social pilgrimage
...and as happy hour
gets near, it's time again for us to reappear...on the scene...so man, let's make
arrangements for some
more good times and fulfill the rest of our day?
Why can't we? Because it's Sunday?
What's so special about the this day, the Lord's day
When we do this every other day?

INTERLUDE

...question of gods...

gods, do ya'll exist?
well some say no.
they argue that gods wouldn't
allow things like wars, pain,
cancer and worldly gains.
but, I argue that
the gods exist in you and
you have to paint the
image of a god for yourself.
But don't
use the wrong type of paint,
'cause the painted
image might not come out.

(37)

Finger Pointing

Mr. blind man...
How do you walk straight into my shadow of doubt?
And vision-less bat...
Why do you continually fly through to my insecurities?
But truck of anguish...
Why are you always in my blind spot
When I jump into your lane,
And I've checked each mirror and never see
you coming?
And unbiased theft...
Why do you always enter my house of blues
And steal my joy and happiness?
But Mr. Anti-cupid...
Why am I always shot with your arrow of hurt?
And Miss Uninvited...
Why do you always find the way to my affection,
Only confronted with rejection?
And you, Mr. blackjack dealer...
Why do you keep handing me aces,
Knowing I'll always lose out?
You especially, disappointment...
You always hit me where
My dreams overflowed?
I don't understand,
Are my weaknesses apparent?
Are my objectives prone to calamity?
Are my aims the bull's eye of the villain's arrow?
Or, is it just...

(38)

That One 'little' Sin

I knew that it was wrong.
But, like always,
I was sure that God would forgive me.
After all,
He forgave me those millions of other times
when I did wrong,
And
I was feeling fine and
Nothing was hindering my mind.
So, I thought,
he wouldn't mind,
If I gave in to temptation
and did something that I
knew I shouldn't do.
Like I said before,
He forgave me those millions of other times.
Before I did it,
In the mist of doing it,
And
After I finished, I felt 100 percent fine.
I didn't even regret what I had done.
And I even contemplated on doing it again.
BUT,
Before I could ask for forgiveness,
Before I could even open my mouth,
It was like lightning struck my body,
And air no longer filled each lung.
It felt like fire filled my blood vessels,
And a bomb exploded upon my tongue.
My plug to life was cut off,
And thrown into a pool of fire.
As my soul burned like a lynched slave,
Was this worth one sinful desire?

(39)

THE PRICE

Part One- The Commitment
He kneeled down to negotiate with His Father and He started to have bitter regrets.
But His father let Him know that this had to be done for the prophecy hadn't fulfilled yet.
Suddenly an angel from heaven appeared,
And provided Him with heavenly power.
And He arose and took a look at His disciples,
And He saw them weeping in sorrow.
The human side of Him wanted to withdraw,
Until His heavenly side said "persist."
He turned with faith engraved in His heart,
And was betrayed by Judas with a kiss.
The disciples knew what
would happen to Jesus so
Peter cut the servant's ear with his sword.
But Jesus touched his
ear and healed him instantly,
But still the servant, wouldn't serve
the Lord.
Another servant asked
"Are you Christ?"
And Jesus said
"Will you not believe if I admit?"
Jesus knew that the servants
would not set him free.
So He grinned and said,
"I will mildly submit!"

Part Two - The Submission
Jesus told them that He was the son of God,
And then respectfully said,
"Yes, Christ is me!"
When the servants heard
those words from his mouth,
The Lord was prepared for all misery.
After the trial of the Lord went to pass,
And the people cried, "Crucify!"
He was taken away by
a great company of men,
But not a tear fell from His eyes.

Jesus comforted the daughters of Jerusalem,
And instructed that for Him not to weep.
Jesus said, "Weep for your children and for yourselves."
As he was led for his expected defeat.
A massive cross was thrown across His back,
As He suffered people stood patiently.
The servants lashed scars across His body,
And then His bones the crowd could see.

Part Three - The Prophecy Fulfills
"Father forgive them for they know not what they do,"
Jesus mourned as the servant pierced His side.
His body began to shake from the immense measure of pain,
As the spectators watched and cried.
The soldiers mocked Jesus and offered him vinegar,
And on His head they put the crown of thorns.
"THE KING OF THE JEWS" was written on the cross,
And the pain consumed the savior as He mourned.
Jesus yelled with a loud and shaky voice and said,
"Father into thy hands I commend my soul."
He gave up His spirit
into the hands of His father,
And this prophecy began to unfold.
He journeyed to the world beneath our world,
During the time that His spirit was set free.
He released those who believed that He was soon to come.
And told them, "Heaven you believers shall see!."
As His earthly body rest beneath a rock,
He had once told them that
He would soon return.
And in three days His body was not in the grave,
And a lesson the non-believers did learn.
Once Jesus returned He saw Mary weeping,
"Where has thy taken my Lord?", she cried.
Jesus smiled and said,
"My child thy seekest me?"
And the tears upon her face were dried.
Jesus gave a brief speech to the believers of Him,
And He said, "Heaven is now waiting for me.
Remember the price I've paid to forgive your sins,
And now, the cost of your salvation, is free."

(40)

the chair

I sit,
in the chair,
on the other side of the room,
and watch you...
on your death bed...
and think, why?
and ask God why?
because, if you die, then...
I'll die...
as I sit...
in the chair,
on the other side of the room,
and watch you...
on your death bed...
with the monitor on your heart...
and "death" calling your name...
but, don't turn your head and look at him...
because if you die, then...
I'll die.
It's sad to look at you trying to smile...
when the doctor's already said,
"You won't be here but for a while...
longer," cause 'death' is calling your name...

but please don't turn your head and look at him...
because if you die, then...
I'll die.

(41)

Last Breath

"...I have just moments to live,
But I'll tell you what I think you should know.
Take good care of the family my son,
Because the time has come for her to go.
I never understood why my Lord,
Delivered me his package of eccentric years.
Filled with memories of triumphs and failures,
And days when her eyes opened with tears.
I gave all the love that I had to give,
And you can say you received an abundant share.
There was never a moment of doubt in your mind,
That I loved you and truly cared.
The pain that her heart endured,
No one will ever appreciate or feel.
But God was my witness to the pain that I suffered,
And your troubles He knows are real.
I feel my soul leaving this earth,
But God shall spare me time to tell...
Remember the legacy I left you,
And child continue to thrive and excel.
I will always love you my heir of eminence,
For it's time for me to dance with death.
Just remember the things that she shared with us, year after year,
As I take my very last breath, breath, breath..."

(42)

For Rent

The empty place in my heart is for rent,
For the one who occupied it last, packed her belongs,
Disappeared without a trace
Which is why this vacant place is looking for a new owner.
I kept her deposit to cover the extensive damage caused
When she moved in, tore up the place,
And left my heart,
An unsuitable place
For any other love to live,
Until someone can give me,
A deal to make me reconsider,
Renting my heart again.

INTERLUDE

...unable to swim...

I'm unable to swim,
so please don't throw me back into
the ocean of misery
the sea of oppression
or the pool of dissension...

(43)

THE diviNG boARd

how can I prepare you?
how can I help you climb
those stairs (and stand to bare)
you jump...and dive deep...
deep into disparity -
a disparity that I've experienced,
and still feel -
and understand how terrible and
unreal the pain will feel...
will you lose your head first?
or will you lose everything at once?
or will you fear the fear that lurks
when I push you deep into the pool
of depression...when I know you won't
be able to swim...and will drown in your
hurt and mine as well?

(44)

Who am I?

**I know half of me.
Why couldn't I just be,
The person I wanted to be.
The one I thought I should be.
For that's who I knew as me.
And not be, who I am?
Seven ticks past the ides of March,
Of eight after nine,
The definition of myself,
I could no longer define.
Pain attacking on many levels,
mentally, physically, and spiritually.
But I have to stay strong because you see,
No one knows me.
Do you really know me?
Do I know me?
I don't know!
But I won't let
that stop me from going on.
Still, I can't help but wonder who I am?
Let me think! I know half of me.
But why couldn't I just be
The person I wanted to be.
The one I thought I should be.
For that's who I knew as me.
And not be, Who I am?**

(45)

Un-Like

Un-like others, getting some is not my aim,
I don't care if you or others label me "lame,"
Getting drunk will never be my "thang"
Because I don't have to be like anyone else,
- not a single soul -
Whether I'm digging myself in a hole,
Seeking a higher goal, or even taking a voyage through my soul,
I will always be un-like everyone.
But un-like some people,
you shouldn't un-like me for my un-likeness.

...asilook at our lineage given...
...asilook at being lost and confused...
...asilook at the costs of liability...
...asilook at the women we mustn't abuse...

(46)

Coma

Tried to forget
And it's something you'll always regret.
The pain hurts I bet.
It's like you walked in a coma,
Couldn't speak, Couldn't reveal,
But you could think and feel
The pain and life that you tried to forget,
Are something you'll always regret.
You can't miss something you never had,
But it must make you mad,
And I know that you were sad
that you walked around in a coma
and don't remember anything,
not a simple thing,
even the creation date,
and you learned too late
that the pain and life that you tried to forget,
are something that you'll always regret.

(47)

Father, Mother, Parent

A Father...is strong,
And will stand up when you need someone.
A Parent...is easygoing,
But can't relate to their little one.
A Mother...is wise,
And understands the thoughts of her child.
A Parent...is unaware,
And can not read behind the smile.
A Father...is responsible,
And tries to educate the child's mind.
A Parent...is standard,
And complains when the child falls behind.
A Mother...gives love,
And takes pride in
watching her child succeed.
A Parent...loves authority,
And when the child wants, it's do to greed.
A Father...gives his all,
So that the child can live the best of life.
A Parent...takes all,
Including their children's pride,
so they can suffice.
A Mother...understands
that you have to respect
the child's personal views.
A Parent...opens his or her hand
On each Friday, to collect the weekly dues.

(48)

Taxi Cab

You opened the door.
You strapped me in.
You drove me away.
And, the cost was more
than what I should
have had
to pay.
You opened the door
I strapped myself in.
You drove me away
I had to provide my own directions
- Despite your fare -
To get to my destination
But you wanted the credit
for taking me there?
I opened the door myself,
I didn't even strap myself in.
Your car ran out of fuel
So I had to provide my own fuel
And find another way - another means of transportation
To reach my destination -
Despite the hindrance and the instigation
You caused - but I still found my way.
Why do I still owe you a fare though?

INTERLUDE

...give me...

give me someone to love,
someone to make me happy,
someone to make love...
someone who will make love last...
some one to make love last forever...
someone who will make love mean something...
someone who will show me she's happy to make our love last forever...
someone who will make me stop writing about wanting someone to love
and make me happy...

(49)

But Then

**My eyes continue to gaze,
Asilook astonished and amazed.
For I see someone full of love,
Perfection in human form from above.
God was showing off when He compiled,
Someone so precious, wonderful, and mild.
As I continue to look at her face,
I think of our future while my heartbeats race.
Then I think of holding her body tight,
And fulfilling her fantasies every night.
Wishing I could hold her for all of time,
Asilook at her smile
with its distinguished shine.
How I crave to hold her oh so near,
For my emotions have shifted
into love's high gear...
but then...
Her current love intrudes between,
And my beautiful sight
becomes a disastrous scene.
For her heart belongs to someone else,
When I wanted her solely for myself.
Oh God how my heart then aches inside,
As the pain and my emotions coincide.
For the love that
I wanted has been proclaimed, and
her innocent heart doesn't feel the same.
The mirage vanished and exposed my fears,
Asilook my eyes are now filled with tears.
Then I think to myself that if she is the one,
Then why haven't our hearts converged as one?
I can't help but think will I ever find,
A woman that has my heart on her mind?**

(50)

??? Un-Answered Questions ???

???

??? When I hold you in my arms
Why does my heart begin to race???
And when I go to sleep every night,
Why do I dream about your face???

???

??? Why haven't I told you I love you,
When all I do is think of you???
Who keeps telling me that
"This is the one that is right for you???"

???

??? Who are you to steal my heart,
and tangle it in your affection???
And why can't I resist your love,
And fill your heart with complete rejection?

???

??? Why do people smile at us,
whenever we walk and hold hands???
And why do I feel this way about you,
Because now, I'm your friend's man???

(51)

Black Woman, You're All Mine

You are the model for the beautiful,
black woman, the diva of the divine.
You are an example waiting to be set,
But most importantly black woman,
You're all mine.
You've got the body that
all clothes are made to fit.
With a personality
That all men can relate with.
You are every woman in one,
The extended definition of fine.
A smile that lights up the galaxy,
But most importantly black woman,
You're all mine.
A convergence of all sweetness,
and a compilation of God's best.
Even when you fail black woman,
You are still considered the success.
You have the voice of
the Choir of Angels,
You are the image
that God had in mind.
You are everything now and forever,
But most importantly black woman,
You're all mine.

(52)

For Your Love

For your love,
I'd climb the highest mountain
to meet you, my love,
on the top.
And the love that we share,
would have so much force,
That the earth's rotation would stop.
For you love,
I'd swim the depths of the seas,
And your charm would
provide light for me to see.
We would show the world our happiness,
And set examples of
what true love should be.
For you love,
I'd travel around the world so I could
hold you forever in my arms.
I'd do all this because I love you,
And promise to protect you from all harm.
For you love, I'd take on the world
And challenge all, even
if my life would be at risk.
I'd do all these things to be next to you,
To feel your touch and loving kiss.

INTERLUDE

...Sanctions...

Limited to do
what we like to do
because us two,
have been limited,
prohibited,
restricted,
and inhibited
To be ourselves
And let the love we truly share
show,
for inside we know
That no sanctions can keep us apart...
For there will always be that invisible chain connecting our hearts

(53)

The Emmy

And the winner goes to...
You - because you played the hell out of the role.
Not only did your performance cause tears,
But it also provoked pain and fear - without horror.
Provoked fear...Of falling apart when your role
took over my screen and sent sounds that rumbled my theater.
Then-as months passed-you made it into my home and had me up
many late nights watching
and anticipating
your next move,
yet thinking about how I would make it through...
the magnitude of your role's dimensions.
So, I went and got my own version
of your drama - and kept you next to me each day,
each moment, and at all times.
But please, please don't thank me.
Thank yourself, although you used my script to play your role.

(54)

The Camera

It captured the writer's success,
and created a goal to defeat.
...it revisited the intense hurt
the writer never wanted to repeat.
...it captures a writer's thoughts,
and freezes them for that term.
...it saved an author's feeling of failure,
and recorded the lesson he learned.
...it caught the mourner's tears...
...it resurfaced the victim's fears...
...reiterated a loser's bet...
...it retrieved the challenges met...
...it revealed the inner part of me...
...it's a form of a lens for me...
...it's a way to discharge and find comfort for me...
...it's the art, the craft, the composition of poetry...

(55)

any

any time, any place,
any one,
any face,
any day,
any groove,
any way,
any move,
any or many
attempts to
sensually please
can lead to
any or many
STDS.

(56)

Cortex

Thoughts of...
"Lying, Cheating,"
"Spousal beating,"
"Individuality,"
"Normality,"
"Try-Sexuality"
Thoughts of...
"Instigation"
"Relations,"
"Masturbation,"
"Why, Die, Wanting to Pry"
Thoughts of...
"Shedding Tears, Inner Fears,"
"Falling apart, Larger parts,"
"Breaking A Heart"
Thoughts of...
"Suicide, Excessive pride,"
"A Different Family,"
"Immorality"
"World Monopoly"
Thoughts of...

INTERLUDE

...x-ray...

okay, you see through me,
but,
can you see right in me?
if not,
keep looking...

...asilook at my search for happiness...
...asilook at my molding and foundation...
...asilook at the point of my words...
...asilook at and give my appreciation...

(57)

Mr. Scary Man

Mr. Scary Man
Why are you so afraid?
Are you afraid to be true,
Afraid to go through,
Afraid to do...
What you're afraid to do?
When I know you
Can, be all that you can
And not have to be
Mr. Scary Man.
What's wrong? you still
Singin' that sad song?
Talkin' bout, how you don't
Wanna go on
when I've told you
What you need to do.
Well, maybe you're afraid...
Afraid to be true,
Afraid to go through,
Afraid to do...
What's you're afraid to do.
'Cause I know you
Can, be all that you can
'Cause you don't have to be
Mr. Scary Man.

(58)

The Familiar Assassin

Everything he says is a lie.
Your assassin's right in your sight.
He watches your every single move,
While contemplating his deadly bite.
He will smile all in your face.
And have the nerves to make you laugh.
If you could only hear
the thoughts of his mind.
Of the things he wants that you have.
You will never know who he is.
He wears an invisible veil.
Since no one knows
when he'll explode and attack,
Be armed and ready with your shield.
Please don't tell him all your secrets,
For he will publicize your life.
When you two become the best of friends,
That's when he reaches for the knife.
You'll start to treat him like your brother,
Then you'll sit back, chill, and relax.
And when the friendship prospers,
He will stab you in the back.

(59)

They Said

They said I was destined to be in jail,
They said I'd backslide and burn in hell.
They said I wouldn't amount to anything,
They said I couldn't write, dance, or sing.
They said I would keep failing and never suc-
ceed.
They said I would be overcome with sin and
greed.
They said I better watch my back.
They said They'd be hard and
wouldn't cut me no slack.
They said before 2 and 1 I'd be dead.
But, I don't give a damn about what
what the hell they said.

(61)

1899

Tonight,
We're gonna party like it's 1899.
We're gonna wave our confederate flags,
And hold on to those days when we could claim
Victory - although we fixed the race.
We're gonna relapse back to the days
When we celebrated the heritage of hate - with pride,
- And forced all efforts of unity,
To halt for another 60 years.
Our ancestors shed blood and tears,
To defend our heritage of hate, time after time,
So, we're gonna have a party
And celebrate,
Like it's 1899.

INTERLUDE

value

it's not conceit,
it's not arrogance,
it's called "value."
one must know his
value in a world where he
is constantly marketing
himself

(62)

TIME

When someone took the time, to see how I utilized my time.
They saw how I've spent so much time, helping others,
Working hard to achieve,
And giving all my talent,
and giving all time, to the world.
Then, that person took the time to tell TIME
of the occupancy of my
time - resulting in TIME taking time to show
The world that it was my time to shine.

(63)

You Always Have A Frien

When your inspiration is gone,
and your mind is discouraged
and you can't find a reason why.
Think of where we've been,
And know my friend,
That I'll provide a shoulder for you to cry.
When your heart is in love,
And you need that help
To make sure that it will never end.
July or December,
Just always remember,
That you always have a friend.
When someone has departed,
in your life,
I will always feel your pain.
A friend 'til death due us part,
Sincerely from my heart,
And never let your esteem take the drain.
When I can't go on,
And need you there by me,
To provide a foundation
with strength and pride.
Don't let me be,
For you know me,
Pour confidence 'til it overflows inside.
When your skies are blue,
And you need that reassurance to make
sure our relationship won't bend.
anytime, anyplace,
any endeavor you face,
Remember, you always have a friend.

(64)

Respectfully Dedication

If only you could have lived to see,
All the capability you foreshadowed in me,
If only you could have been able to live,
In the house and the car I'd one day afford to give.
If only you could be around,
To lighten my day when you saw any frown,
But God said that it was your time to leave...
this world that wasn't fulfilling your spiritual needs...
And give up a life of eternal pain,
To rejoice in paradise with no sign of strain...
therefore,
I can smile knowing that you'd be by my side,
Smiling back at me with eyes overflowing with pride,
And I can feel your presence in all that I do,
For everything, I mean everything I do,
I do it for you.

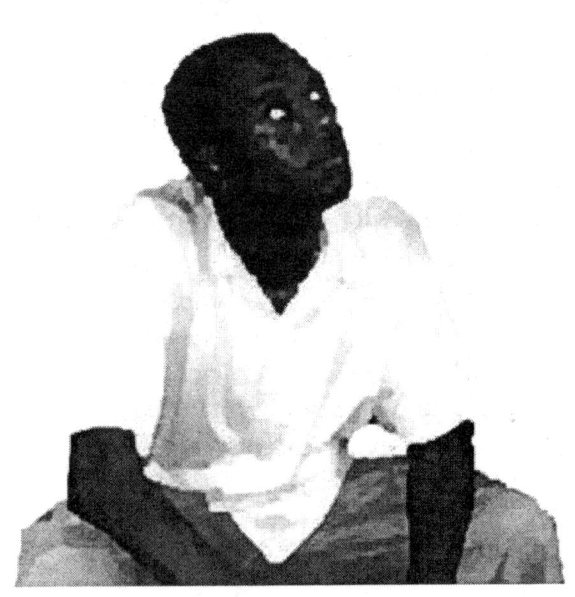

(65)
This Friend, Happiness

My family always talked about this
friend they wanted me to find.
His name - happiness.
He didn't live too far, but he moved around
frequently and consistently changed his image.
But, to contact him, you had
To find his latest number - which varied from man to man.
As a child, I was told that toys and games
would often bring him into my home.
As a result, he stayed at our house for years,
Then in my pre and early teen years,
We moved away from happiness, and it was nearly
Impossible to find his latest number.
Before he departed, he said he didn't know when he
could come back to visit.
Along with him,
went grandma, grandpa
and auntee'.
For awhile, He didn't call, didn't write,
until that one night,
when he stormed in
in a womanly structure.
But, when she came this time,
she carried love and affection -
that turned into hurt, agony,
and when the storm passed on,
a broken heart remained.
As years went by, happiness called and asked
could he come stay with me for awhile
- until he got back on his feet.
Naive and confused,
I told him he could stay.
However, when he came this time,
He brought a suitcase filled with
Deliverance and joy and a night bag with a bottle of peace it in.
And next to his heart,
He brought a child named
Jesus, that he held close to his heart.

(66)

...asilook...

**As I look,
I may - or may not - see the uniqueness,
the meekness, the originality,
The humility...
But, As I look,
I'm confused on whether his thoughts are
just poetic interpretations,
Or personal complications and situations.
But whether he's 120 miles away or orating on
how one equals two.
Deep within, he wants
his work to be apart of you.
As I look further in, I get a glimpse of a healing soul.
But beneath the bandages,
the wounds are covered with
Encouragement and dedication to every goal.
As I Look, I notice that like many people -
He has a heart willing to love,
Willing to care, and resources and
Assurance that he's wants to share.
Still, in the mist of distress,
he aims hard to keep his foundation,
and is active in the revolution for our people, within this nation,
and standing in the mist, with his fist up high,
and realizes that all blessings have roots up high...
Whether or not he has wounds or is crying "Ohh God,"
he will always have access to the golden rod.
And with help from God,
- who paid the price -
he has received the directions
to the everlasting life,
As I look, at this dynamic man I see,
I realize, that I'm looking,
right in the mirror.
And this dynamic, rational,
capable, reliable, humble,
God fearing,
and
conquer-less man,
is the reflection of "me."
work and progress.**

FINALE

...the hibernation...

life is dyin', Folks a cryin,
my mental clock is tryin'
to drop me a hint that
its time to close
my eyes,
and rest.
as I close my eyes,
and stop looking,
you,
close your eyes,
and rest with me...and let us return,
when the "resurrection" occurs,
when the "emergence" transpires,
when the "rekindling" begins,
and we'll return stronger than ever,
and re-surface with more images,
again...

...ABOUT THE AUTHOR...

Mark Anthony Thomas was born on August 9, 1979, to Ernest and Veronica Thomas in Big Rapids, Michigan. As the middle child, in 1990 his family relocated to Stone Mountain, Georgia and he attended and graduated from Redan High School in 1997. Shortly after graduating from high school, he was named the 1997 Atlanta Braves/ Principal Health Care English Scholar of the Year. In fall 1997, he enrolled at the University of Georgia and majored in Marketing and Mass Communications. He began writing for the Red & Black independent student newspaper in September 1997 – the daily campus newspaper at the University of Georgia. On April 25, 1998, he was initiated into the Zeta Pi Chapter of Alpha Phi Alpha Fraternity, Inc. In addition to the fraternity, Thomas also began making contributions to the Upward Bound and Communiversity Programs. In 1999, he was selected to serve as one of the official campus ambassadors with the Arch Society and in March 1999, he was named the Editor-In-Chief of the Red & Black – becoming the first African American to hold the position in the newspaper's 106-year history. In addition to the Red & Black, his works have also appeared in the Infinite Greek Magazine, Atlanta Journal-Constitution, and Ebonylove.Net. In August 1999, he appeared in Time Magazine's "2000 Best Colleges For You" guide – as one of the magazine's student profiles. In November 1999, Thomas was selected as the Alpha Phi Alpha Fraternity Georgia District College Brother of the Year. In addition, in February 1999, he won the Frank Green Southern Region Service Award for his fraternity. That same month, Thomas was featured on Atlanta's NBC Affiliate – 11-Alive – as one of the station's "Future Black History Makers of Tomorrow." During the summer of 2000, Thomas worked for Telemate.Net Software, Inc. as the company's Marketing and Public Relations Intern. "As I Look" is Thomas' first book and he also maintains several web pages. He is a dedicated member of Holy Fellowship C.O.G.I.C. in Decatur, GA.